Being Desperate and Living Uniquely for the Gospel

Witness Lee

Living Stream Ministry
Anaheim, California • www.lsm.org

First Edition, January 1987.

ISBN 0-87083-272-7 (large)

Published by

Living Stream Ministry
2431 W. La Palma Ave., Anaheim, CA 92801 U.S.A.
P. O. Box 2121, Anaheim, CA 92814 U.S.A.

Printed in the United States of America

00 01 02 03 04 05 / 12 11 10 9 8 7 6 5 4 3

CONTENTS

PREFACE

This book is comprised of messages given by Brother Witness Lee in Anaheim, California in January 1987.

CHAPTER ONE

DOOR-KNOCKING AND FRUIT-BEARING

Scripture Reading: John 15:2, 4, 16a; Matt. 21:34, 43

POSITIVE RESULTS OF THE LORD'S NEW WAY FOR HIS NEW MOVE

Since October of 1984 the Lord has been speaking to us concerning His new way for His new move. We have gained much understanding in these last one and a half years in Taipei and have found out the sure way to gain the increase. Within the past three months, seven hundred full-time trainees in Taipei baptized over seven thousand new believers and set up over two thousand new home meetings. In over five hundred and twenty of these homes, the whole household got saved. Despite this success, I cannot say I am fully satisfied because my budget was that seven hundred would baptize seven hundred each week. This means that every week one full-time trainee should get one baptized. That would have yielded two thousand eight hundred a month and eleven thousand two hundred baptized in four months.

The main reason we did not reach this goal was that we did not have our training facility quite prepared when the training began. Our work on a lodging place took away some of our time. Also, in the training we did not have enough experience to know how to motivate the trainees in the way that a coach trains athletes. One full-time trainee from Malaysia baptized one hundred and twenty, and another brother from the United States baptized one hundred and twenty-six. On the one hand, the trainers in Taipei were very happy to get over seven thousand baptized. But on the other hand, I am not fully satisfied because I wanted to get over eleven thousand. In this next phase of the training with the proper coaching, I believe we will go over our budget for the increase. It is still wonderful, however, that within a short time, over seven thousand were baptized and over two thousand new home meetings were set up in one city. On the day of Pentecost, three thousand were added and later "the number of the men came to about five thousand" (Acts 4:4). This proves that the new way the Lord has given us for His new move really works.

Recently, I have been receiving letters, not only from different states, but also from different countries, encouraging me to encourage the saints to take this new way. To talk about going this new way is easy. To practice the new way is also easy if you have the heart. With the practice of the new way, "if there is a will, there is a way."

I recently received an encouraging letter from a certain local church in the United States of about sixty saints. A leading brother there wanted to let me know how the Lord has been blessing their door-knocking since they began to take the trained way of one out of four saints knocking on doors for two to three hours a week. After last summer's training, they began going out door-knocking. On the Lord's Day morning after the truth lesson, the saints would haphazardly break into groups and go out to knock on doors in whatever part of the city they desired. He said that this proved to be unsuccessful because their method was loose, and they were not strict in applying the new way. In light of the five messages given in August of 1986 *(The New Way to Carry Out the Increase and Spread of the Church)* and after receiving much fellowship from the full time training in Taipei, they turned to take a much stricter way with the door-knocking.

In October they had the saints sign up to be on a team and to make a definite consecration to give two hours each week for the door-knocking. Over half of the church signed up. The ratio was exactly two sisters to each brother for groups of three saints. They assigned the saints to specific teams and assigned the teams to specific areas in the city. Each team, composed of two door-knocking groups, was charged to go out on a weekly basis to follow strict procedures of the new way and to keep detailed records of their activities for statistical purposes. This brother pointed out in his letter that although the outward practices have to be preceded by the inward filling of the Spirit, it seems that the Lord will bless the outward practices of the new way if they are strictly applied. He said that in their experience, the stricter the practice was, the greater the anointing was. The difference they experienced when they turned from the loose way to the strict way was marvelous. The saints were once again stirred and motivated about the door-knocking. The anointing was with them. Homes were being opened, and people were being baptized.

Even though the saints in this locality were all involved in the winter training this year in Irving, some of the teams were still going out, and ten were baptized during the training. One team went out one day during the training, and six were baptized in less than an hour and a half. During the training, more saints were stirred up to go out for the door-knocking, and now about seventy percent of the saints in this small church of about sixty saints have signed up for the one in four trained door-knocking. One of the full-timers there returned from Taipei in December, and now with him they will have an intensive weekend door-knocking training.

The leading brother in this local church wanted me to know that they were very burdened to stand with me in prayer for the success of steps two, three, and four in Taipei: knowing the truth and teaching the truth to the new converts in their homes; growing in life to minister life; and having the practice of the church life in the homes. This church registered six for the full-time training in Taipei this spring, leaving two full-timers there. That makes eight full-timers out of a church of sixty. In May, four more of their saints will be graduating, and they also plan to go full-time. They and many others of the students there are consumed with the desire to go full-time.

I also received another letter from a couple who returned to another locality from the full-time training in Taipei. They began to go out each evening to knock on doors with the saints there and were encouraged with the saints' eagerness to come with them to learn how the training taught them to knock on doors and to enter into the new way. A leading brother in this locality who went with this couple to knock on doors one evening, baptized a friend of his son in the new way in his home the following day. This brother testified that if he had not gone out to knock on doors, this would not have happened. Now this brother is "catching on fire" and wants to grasp every opportunity to go out with this couple.

They began to visit the apartments surrounding the meeting hall and of the one hundred and one doors knocked on in four evenings, sixty doors opened, and seventeen of these were entered. Of the twenty-five people they contacted, nine were genuine sisters. Eleven prayed and received the Lord, and they had one glorious baptism. This newly baptized sister was so happy that she did not have to "go to church" to be baptized. Her words were, "That's great!" Afterward, she expressed how grateful she was that the saints came, and she wanted to know whose idea it was to visit people in their homes. They told her that it was the Lord's idea. They now have a total of eleven homes that are open to them to revisit for a home meeting. This couple testified that they love the new way and that the new way is satisfying, reviving, encouraging, and refreshing. It has brought them the experience of joy unspeakable.

Up to the last week of the training in Taipei, the full timers there had baptized only a little over six thousand. They felt this number was not up to the standard, so within the last week of the training they got close to one thousand. They baptized such a large number within one week because they became desperate. Two heretical groups, the Mormons and the Jehovah's Witnesses, also knock on doors, but we do not follow them. If you have enjoyed and still enjoy going to visit people by knocking on their doors, you know there is a big difference.

DROPPING THE OLD WAY AND TAKING THE NEW WAY

Beginning in October of 1984, I began to express my concern about the low rate of increase in the churches. In Taipei we had come to a standstill. When I left Taipei in 1961, the total number of saints in the church in Taipei was over twenty-two thousand. By 1984 the church in Taipei had only eleven thousand members left. Within twenty-three years the number came down to eleven thousand. In the last ten years in the United States, due to the defamation of some books, the rate of our increase has been just about three percent. This is too low. After studying our situation, I began to reconsider the Bible in this matter, and I also began to reconsider the history of the denominations. I became clear that all of Christianity, including us, got off from the Lord's way. Thus, I was quite bold in Taipei to tell them that they must change by getting off the old way, and getting on the new way.

The old way is to always have big meetings, a congregation with a speaker. This produces clergy, a hierarchical class with most of the others not functioning. Taking the way of a big congregation with a speaker produces hierarchy and also produces organization. The organizational way is to have clergy and a congregation and to raise up money to hire trained preachers. People are first brought into this way, and then their function is killed. This is the way of Christianity. Brother Nee told us repeatedly and insisted strongly that we give up the Lord's Day morning meeting in the churches. He proposed that we use that time to go out to preach the gospel. In Brother Nee's book, *The Normal Christian Church Life,* there is a section on the home meetings (pp. 195-200). He told us that we needed to have meetings of mutuality, not meetings where one speaks and the other saints sit there to listen. We tried this, but we never carried it out because of the heavy background and influence from Christianity.

The situation in Taipei in 1984 was nearly the same as what was practiced by Christianity. Therefore, I had the boldness to tell the church there that the old way should be put aside, and that they should take the new way according to what is in the Bible. At the very beginning of the church life, according to the first record of Christian meetings, the apostles spoke in the temple to a big congregation for the preaching of the truth, yet the believers met "from house to house" (Acts 2:46). In Greek this means that they met according to the houses. Each and every house was a meeting place;

the meeting number was according to the houses. After the day of Pentecost when they were baptized, they met according to the homes. They did not have hired speakers, but they had the church life in their homes. They also met in the temple, but this was according to their tradition and habit and not according to God's economy. That was not the church life.

The more we studied the situation according to the truth of the New Testament and according to our experience, the more we were assured that the right way is to have the church life built up in the homes. First Corinthians 14 talks about the whole church coming together in one place (v. 23). But this is not a meeting of only a few speakers but a meeting in which "each one has" (14:26), a meeting full of mutuality. The old Christianity way of one speaking and the others sitting to listen kills the church life.

In the full-time training in Taipei, I told the trainers not to bring the new ones to the church meetings. Occasionally, some new ones asked the trainees to bring them to a church meeting. After one or two church meetings, these new ones said they did not want to go to the church meeting again. They liked to enjoy the meeting in the homes. They did not have a taste for the big meetings. But with many of us it is exactly the opposite. We have a taste for the big meetings. When you bring your contacts to a meeting, you may like to have a big hall, a large congregation, and a big, eloquent speaker. All of this is a good facade. We have been meeting in this way in our localities for many years, and what has been the result? We have had hardly any increase, but instead have been maintaining a traditional Christian worship service. People today are quarreling, debating about doctrine and about different practices in Christianity, but I am not burdened merely for the doctrines or for practices. I only care for the New Testament faith, the Christian faith, the New Testament economy. As long as we have this, let us take the new way to have the increase.

According to the statistics of religious bodies in the United States, eight large denominations have decreased in their membership—the United Methodists, the Presbyterians, The

Lutheran Church in America, the Episcopalians, The Lutheran Church—Missouri Synod, the American Lutherans, the United Church of Christ, and the Churches of Christ. The Assemblies of God have increased, yet by only six percent a year. This increase of the Assemblies of God is the highest. The second is the United Pentecostals with a 4.8 percent increase per year. The yearly percentage of increase for the Roman Catholic Church in the United States is only .68 percent. This confirmed that the way of Christianity does not work well.

Nevertheless, we have been and are still under the influence of Christianity. To some extent we follow them. Sixty years ago at the beginning of the Lord's recovery in China, we mostly followed the Brethren way, but the number of Plymouth Brethren in the United States is only ninety-eight thousand. This is much too low a number. The entire way of Christianity does not work well. Could we be satisfied to have a six percent yearly increase? We must take the new way! And the new way has been practiced and fully proven: it works. Over seven thousand were baptized in Taipei within less than four months. The brother from that local church of sixty told us that six were baptized by one team within an hour and a half. This is according to our training. We present them the truth in a quick way with no vain talk, and we believe in the Lord's word concerning baptism.

Our practice has proven that the proper baptism by water really works out something. One brother knocked on a certain door and the man who answered said he was not interested. Then the brother went to the back door, the kitchen door, and knocked. The man told the brother again that he was not interested. The brother then said to the man, "Since you will not allow me to come in, please come out." That man took the order and came out. This brother read to him a short paragraph from *The Mystery of Human Life* and that man got baptized. Many were like this. After being baptized, they became happy. They were changed.

There is power in the proper baptism. Baptism is not a ritual, but we have made it a ritual by our practice. Many times we would wait weeks or months before we baptized someone. That kind of baptism became a ritual. But the present new way is that we baptize people immediately after they believe (Acts 8:35-38; 16:14-15, 33-34; 22:16; Mark 16:16). After they pray, we direct them to be baptized in their bathtub. Many of those baptized in the new way experienced a real change and came up out of the water to walk in newness of life (Rom. 6:4).

Many of us have become drugged with the old way of having big meetings. When we made the change from having the big meetings in the hall to having the small meetings in the homes, many saints were disappointed. But the newly baptized ones like the home meetings. Some brothers in Taipei got addicted to the home meetings, and many trainees got addicted to the baptism in the new way. If they could not get one baptized every evening, they felt they were short. They got addicted to this practice and found that to baptize people in faith is a real joy. These new ones are growing. They have begun to seek after the Lord and to know the truth.

Many of us have become drugged. We are too satisfied with the old way to have a congregation. But I have seen a view that perhaps after five years in Taipei, the church will just be meeting in many homes. Now in Taipei they have four hundred old home meetings plus the over two thousand new home meetings. We are going to have another term of training, and I believe this term will bring in more than three thousand home meetings. Then by the summer of 1987, the church in Taipei will have about six thousand home meetings. Every home will be meeting, every home will be working, every home will be teaching, and every home will be preaching. What spiritual giant can replace six thousand home meetings with the entire household functioning?

Our way to baptize people and gain homes is wonderful. Sometimes the husband got baptized and the next week his wife believed. Our trainees then directed the husband to baptize his wife, and the husband baptized his wife! The bathtubs in Taiwan are not so big, so the ones who were baptized had to be immersed and have the water sprinkled and poured upon them at the same time. The water in the bathtub was not that much, but the Spirit was so much! Often when our trainees were talking to the husband, the wife resigned with the husband that they would go to the rest room to prepare the water for baptism, even though the wife was not saved yet. When they baptized the husband, they all prayed, "We baptize you into the Triune God!" Some fathers baptized their sons in the week following their own baptism. This is all new. After these household baptisms, these houses began to meet. What a wonderful taste in the home meetings! This is a different taste from the practice of today's Christianity. We have been drugged with the way of Christianity, so a taste of the way of Christianity has been built up within us. We need to take the new way to get another taste.

Furthermore, we have not had much feeling about our years of barrenness in which we did not bring forth much fruit. One leading brother told me that he did not bring anyone to the Lord for twenty years. However, after he began to practice door-knocking in the new way, he baptized seventeen within four months.

My burden is to wake you up because you have been drugged. The Lord says that as a branch, you have to bear fruit. This is serious. If you do not bear fruit, there is the danger that you will be cut off (John 15:2, 6). The words of the Lord in John 15 indicate that as branches of the vine we must bear fruit. If you abide in Him, you will surely bear fruit (15:4). God even took away His kingdom from Israel because Israel was barren, fruitless, and gave His kingdom to another people, the church (Matt. 21:43; Luke 13:6-9). But how about today's church? Who is bearing fruit?

Thirty-eight years ago, when I left mainland China, there were a little over three million Christians. Then the Communists took over the country, and they tore down Christianity. The organizations were closed. Since 1970, the Lord began to use the young men born under communism. Many of them were in their twenties. They picked up the gospel which we and other Christians had sown there, and they became prevailing.

I checked with some experts who researched the Christians' situation on mainland China, and I asked how many

Christians there are today in mainland China. I was told that although Hong Kong newspapers reported thirty million, their research said there were fifty million. Today there are only about seventy-four million Protestant Christians in the United States, the biggest Christian country on this earth. The founders, the forefathers, of this country were all Christians. The Protestants have only increased by about nine million over twenty years since 1964, but within about fifteen years, the increase in mainland China has been about forty-seven million. A good number of these are taking the way of the Lord's recovery. Who did this? There were no chapels, cathedrals, ministers, or pastors. The gospel was preached mostly by pure Christian young people with no clergy, no hierarchy, and no organization. Therefore, all the clergy, hierarchy, and organization needs to be torn down.

Do you not think we have clergy? Do you not think we have hierarchy? We do not call anyone a pastor, but actually we have "pastors." We have followed Christianity's way unconsciously. We brought people in and we killed their function by our way. We say we do not control, but in many respects we do control. The leading ones need to ask themselves if they are part of the clergy and the hierarchy among us. Let us all drop the old way, "the old coat!" I am not only telling the elders to drop "the old coat." All of the older generation must give up the taste of the old way and take the new taste of the new way. For the Lord's sake, we need to take the new taste.

In another two years, I believe the Lord will raise up a strong model in Taipei. Among the new ones recently baptized in Taipei, close to one hundred will be full-timers. Some of them told the trainees right after their baptism: "You are a full-timer saving me. I'd like to be a full-timer saving others." Do you believe that saving a person is that hard? Do we need to call a big gospel meeting and beg people to come? Do we need to have so-called feasts to invite people? Where are the people? Why would we not go to their homes and bring them "food to go"? If they come to our meeting, we owe them something, but when we go to them, they owe us something (Luke 10:7).

The Lord Jesus was not sitting in the heavens sending out invitations, inviting people to come to Him. He came down out of heaven (John 6:41) to visit Zaccheus's home (Luke 19:5). Then He said, "Salvation has come to this house" (v. 9). He went to Jacob's well, and waited for a Samaritan woman (John 4:6-7). Why would we not follow Him? Why would we just follow Christianity, set up a church building, and be one of the hierarchies, inviting people and learning to speak eloquent things to attract people? Then once they are attracted by you and come to your meetings, they become dead Christians without any function. They may only pull out their checkbook and write some checks to support you in your hierarchy. I am not only talking about Christianity but about us. I believe that after two or three years of our taking the new way, the elders who remain in the old way will be jobless. A brother who wants to be a good speaker with a congregation will not have one since the church life will be in the homes. All the elders and co-workers must learn to knock on doors! The elders must take the lead in this matter.

Due to the urgent need, we are changing the subject of our summer training of 1987 from the Life-study on Leviticus to have a training on the new way of the Lord's new move. I cannot go out to visit many places in many countries, and many saints all over the world have been stirred up to take the Lord's new way. Thus, we will have a training in the United States for ten days, and this will be recorded on video tape which will go out to all the local churches.

Eventually in the recovery, the way of Christianity with a big congregation and one gifted speaker will be completely annulled. For one to minister the Word depends upon whether he has the real burden of some of the truths from the Lord. Such a person is like Paul, who went to Troas and on the Lord's Day, after the breaking of the bread, spoke the word to build up the saints there (Acts 20:6-7). This is not like today's pastors giving sermons week by week. Some of us have been giving people messages week by week for years, but what has been the result? I would not say there is no result, but the rate of the result is too low.

We have tasted the old way, we have experienced the old

way, and we have suffered from the old way. Now many of us have tasted the Lord's new way, which is so sweet and so workable. What would you choose? We have been drugged without bearing fruit in the old way for years, yet we did not have any feeling about it. We came to the big meetings year after year with hardly any new ones brought to the Lord. How could we be satisfied? Let us forget about the old way. When a house gets too old, it should be condemned. You need to get a new house to replace it. I was unhappy with our low rate of increase for the last ten years, but I could not do anything. At that time I was so busy in the Life-study of the New Testament until October of 1984 when I was finally able to return to Taiwan for the sake of the Lord's new way.

THE LORD'S MINISTRY TODAY

The Lord's ministry today is not to build up big congregations. It is to build up the saints in the new way which involves: 1) Learning how to knock on doors, how to touch people with the high gospel within a short time, how to baptize them not only in water but also into the Triune God, and how to set up meetings in their homes. 2) Learning how to feed them the truths concerning the Triune God, concerning life, concerning Christ, and concerning the church, which means we have to learn how to teach the truths in homes. 3) Learning how to help all the new ones to grow in life. 4) Learning how to bring them into the full knowledge and practice of the church, the Body of Christ. This will be done not only by me or by some of you; this will be done by everyone. Every door-knocker will learn this.

After two or three years the saints will have another taste. They will tell you that they do not like to have the big meetings. They like to have the home meetings where they could preach the gospel by themselves and where they could teach the truths by themselves. They will not need any kind of organization. What elders have been in mainland China for the past fifteen years? You may say that is a mess, but I am glad for that "mess." I like to see this kind of "mess." If there could be such a "mess," after fifteen years another fifty million will be converted. This would be wonderful.

The big denominations, the Methodists, Presbyterians, Lutherans, and Episcopalians, have all decreased and are still decreasing according to a recent article. Are we still happy to remain in this degraded situation? Will we not wake up? We should not talk about others, but consider ourselves and drop our old way. I have no interest to take care of the work in the old way. I realize that the old way is the killing way. Would we be happy to remain in this kind of work? I like to see homes. I like this word "home"—home sweet home. My dream is home meetings. The homes are the basic foundation for the building up of the local churches, not the halls with big congregations. When the saints rise up to go out knocking on doors, they will get addicted to knocking on doors, addicted to baptizing people in bathtubs, and addicted to home meetings and to teaching people in home meetings. They will not care for having big meetings in the meeting hall. They have been meeting in the old way for years and many are bored of the old way of meeting. All the elders need to be door-knocking elders. They need to take the lead to go door-knocking. May the Lord grant us all the mercy to completely drop the old way and to fully pick up the Lord's new way.

CHAPTER TWO

QUALIFICATIONS OF DOOR-KNOCKING FOR FRUIT-BEARING

1. Aggressive desperation: John 15:2a; Matt. 25:24-30; 2 Tim. 4:1-2
2. Absolute consecration: Rom. 12:1
3. Uninterrupted abiding in the Lord: John 15:4-5
4. Full saturation with the word: Col. 3:16
5. Prayer for the filling of both the essential and economical Spirit: Acts 11:24; 4:31
6. Going with the authority of Christ: Matt. 28:18-19

An important portion of the Word related to door-knocking for fruit-bearing is in Luke 10. Verses 3 through 6 say, "Go on your way; behold, I send you as lambs in the midst of wolves. Do not carry a purse, nor a bag, nor sandals; and greet no one on the way. And into whatever house you enter, first say, Peace to this house. And if a son of peace is there, your peace shall rest upon it; but if not, it shall return upon you." In these verses the Lord told the seventy that He sent them out as lambs in the midst of wolves. Then He gave them instructions not to carry a purse, a bag, or sandals and not to greet anyone on the way. Also, He told them what to say first when they entered a house. They were not supposed to say, "How are you?" but "Peace to this house."

The son of peace in verse 6 is the very God-chosen and predestinated one. Among so many people, this one is a son of peace predestinated by God. Now God has sent you to gain this one. If a son of peace is there, your peace shall rest upon him. The trainees who were there in Taipei saw and experienced this. They saw many sons of peace upon whom their peace rested. Verse 7 says, "And remain in the same house, eating and drinking the things from them; for the worker is worthy of his wages." You do not owe them; they owe you something. In Taipei some have tasted this experience already. The visited ones eventually prepared lunch for our trainees. The way of door-knocking—visiting people—was first invented by the Lord Jesus.

The burden of this chapter is embodied in the following six points, which are the qualifications of door-knocking for fruit-bearing: aggressive desperation, absolute consecration, uninterrupted abiding in the Lord, full saturation with the word, prayer for the filling of both the essential and economical Spirit, and going with the authority of Christ. If you are such a person who would pick up the new way and do it according to the trained way, I assure you that you will have a big success. The old way and influence of Christianity among us will be overcome.

1. AGGRESSIVE DESPERATION

For years many of us have been drugged persons. A person who is drugged is numb. He does not have any feeling. Some of us did not bear any fruit for twenty years, yet still felt that we were okay. Many of the churches have been under a drugged situation for years. We all have been meeting in our localities week after week and year after year with hardly any increase. We need to be warned to wake up. We have been wrong. Any branch that does not bear fruit will be cut off (John 15:2, 6). Is this not serious?

We have talked much concerning abiding in John 15. But have we entered into the reality of abiding in John 15, and do we realize the seriousness of not bearing fruit? To take a branch away from a tree is serious. After being taken away, the branch loses everything of the tree. You may still be meeting in the name of Christ and have no realization that you have been taken away already. In this fellowship, I do not care for the expounding or interpreting of the Lord's word in John 15. Rather, I hope you would be impressed with the seriousness of not bearing fruit. Any branch that bears no fruit will be taken away. You may have been taken away unconsciously already under your drugged situation. You may say that you enjoy Christ, but where is the enjoyment if you have not borne fruit and have been cut off from the vine tree? How could you enjoy the vine tree? This is solemn. We all have to see how much we have been fooled and drugged by the tradition, the background, and the surrounding of today's Christianity. Millions of Christians are drugged, but we have to be different.

Saints, wake up! As a brother among you, I am shouting, sounding, and even crying to you—you have to wake up! If the Lord is real and the Bible is a true book, it is solemn and serious to be a Christian without bearing fruit. You may have been cut off, taken away, already. This is why you may not have had any enjoyment of Christ for years. You got cut off from Him. The elders and co-workers need to consider this. We may have been in the Lord's recovery for many years, but what have we been doing? We may have been carrying out things in a drugged way, and we may even be drugging others.

Have you ever seen a fruit tree in an orchard that did not bear fruit year after year? Would the husbandman still keep that tree? He would not just cut off the branches, but uproot the entire tree. God intended to uproot Israel because Israel did not bear fruit for years (Luke 13:6-9). How about the church today? Look at today's Christianity. Four of the five major denominations in Protestant Christianity are decreasing in number. These are the Episcopalian, Lutheran, Presbyterian, and Methodist denominations. Only the Southern Baptists are increasing, but their rate of increase is still very low—only about 1.4 percent yearly. The rate of increase among the Assemblies of God runs first only at six percent yearly, while the United Pentecostals have had an increase of less than five percent yearly. This is still too low.

In the past twenty-three years the highest rate of increase we had was around forty percent. But in the last ten years since we suffered from the defamation of some books, our yearly rate of increase has dropped to about three percent. We have blamed the opposition and have taken the excuse of the opposition for our barrenness, but do you believe that with the apostles there was no opposition? Why would we not wake up to do something? It is time for all of us to wake up, especially the elders and co-workers. We must take another way.

Recently the Cleveland area called a gathering for those who had been in the full-time training in Taipei to train some of the other full-timers and anyone available to go. For three days fifty saints went out, and they baptized over forty. Saints, wake up! There is a way. Do not think that there is no way. Thank the Lord that He has shown us the way. Fifty saints going out and baptizing over forty people within three days should be enough to wake up all of us. Would we remain in a drugged situation? If I were one of the elders or co-workers, I would tell the saints that from now on I will go out to knock on doors morning and evening, every day of the week. Our main work from now on is to knock on doors. If you went out in such a desperate way, do you not think you could gain one per day?

To have aggressive desperation, you have to be "crazy." If a person is in a burning building and is desperate for his life, he will jump out of the window. If we do not get someone baptized within a short period of time, we need to be desperate to "jump out of the window," to do anything and everything it takes to get someone baptized. Why would we not go out in this way? All the elders need to "go on strike" from their congregation and go out to knock on doors. Then every home you gain will be a "chapel." After one year, you can set up one hundred "chapels." Some of the homes you go to may even prepare a dinner for you. The trainees in Taipei reported that some homes even gave them gifts. They felt that they owed the saints something.

Saints, wake up! Now is the time. The elders need to realize that the church is not theirs. The church is the church of God (1 Cor. 10:32), the church of Christ (Rom. 16:16), and the church of the saints (1 Cor. 14:33b). If the saints will not fire you as their "pastor," you need to fire yourself by the new way. Blessed are all the elders who fully give themselves to go door-to-door. The elders should leave some of the prayer meetings and the Lord's table meetings to the saints and go to knock on doors. After a month of going door-to-door, you can have the Lord's table in the homes you gain. The elders need to go to create the increase, and their wives need to give up all their opinions and follow their husbands to knock on doors. You do not need to close the hall. The hall is not yours. It belongs to the saints. Just go to knock on doors. You can gain sixty within a short time and have the Lord's table with these new ones in their homes. Where there is a will, there is a way. Do not say there is no way; there is a way, and the Lord has shown us the way. He has dedicated this way; He has cut this way.

Matthew 25:14-30 is a parable for faithfulness. The slothful slave seemingly did not do anything wrong. He did not lose anything. What the Lord gave him, he kept throughout all the years until the Lord came back (v. 25). He even gave the Lord a message pointing out that the Lord was a hard man, reaping where He did not sow and gathering where He did not scatter (v. 24). Did the Lord justify him? He did not. Right away the Lord condemned him. He said, "Evil and slothful slave, you knew that I reap where I did not sow, and gather where I did not scatter. You ought therefore to have deposited my silver with the bankers, and when I came I would have recovered what is mine with interest" (vv. 26-27). The slothful slave should have taken the Lord's word solemnly. He was not desperate. Just to keep what the Lord gave you is not sufficient. He wants the interest, the fruit.

These are some solid verses in the New Testament concerning our destiny. Do you believe the Lord is real? Do you believe He will come back? Do you believe one day He will ask you to give an account? Why are you not solemn? Why are you not serious? Why are you not desperate? Will you just keep what the Lord gave you, not go back to the world, and stay away from sin? You may be a good Christian coming to all the church meetings and keeping all that the Lord has given you. But in this parable the Lord says He wants to recover what is His with interest. This should be enough to cause us to be desperate. Do not say it is too hard, that the opposition is so prevailing. This is just an excuse. This is like telling the Lord He is a hard man, reaping where He did not sow and gathering where He did not scatter. You may take this excuse, but the Lord will never take it. The Lord will take your excuse as a condemnation to you. It is quite possible that we could be this slothful servant.

Paul said that he solemnly charged Timothy by the Lord's appearing and His kingdom (2 Tim. 4:1). His appearing is seen in Matthew 25 with the slothful slave. The kingdom is a kingdom of reward or punishment according to what we have been and what we have done since we were saved until He comes back. In 2 Timothy 4:8 Paul says that he will be awarded with the crown of righteousness by the Lord, the righteous Judge. Paul seriously warned and charged Timothy, not by love nor by kindness, but by the Lord's appearing and by His kingdom. You will be either rewarded or be punished by the righteous Judge righteously at His appearing. This is serious.

Since I saw this fifty years ago, I began to be serious. This seriousness has kept me many times from backsliding and from being slothful. One day He will see me and I will meet Him. In His appearing, I have to give Him an account, and He will decide whether I will receive a reward or a punishment in the coming kingdom. It is a solemn thing. Do not think it is all right if you do not bear fruit for years. I hope this word will stir up your aggressive desperation. As a human being, I must believe in the Lord Jesus; as one of His believers, I must love Him; and as one who loves Him, I must bear fruit. This is serious. No need to say at His coming, at His appearing, even today if I do not bear fruit He will cut me off, take me away from all His riches, from all His supply, from all His enjoyment. Then at His coming I will surely suffer loss (1 Cor. 3:15). I will have to suffer punishment for one thousand years in the manifestation of the kingdom.

2. ABSOLUTE CONSECRATION

The second qualification is to consecrate our body (Rom. 12:1) to go out to visit people by knocking on their doors. This surely needs your body. You may have offered yourself to the Lord many times in prayer, but your prayer may not have issued in a practical consecration of your body. What is the practical consecration of your body to the Lord? It is to bear fruit. As a branch you should not be occupied by anything. You should be pruned. Get away from all the preoccupations that you could be spared and completely unoccupied to bear fruit. I do not mean that you have to drop your job or forget about your living. We have to have a job to make a living. Just spend the amount of time and ability needed to make a living. Do not have any intent to make more money to make yourself rich. Forget about that. That will preoccupy your body from bearing fruit. All of us can spare some time for the sake of bearing fruit. We do not need to work more than what is necessary to make an adequate living. Why do you need to work more so that you can drive a more expensive car? Could you not save some time to knock on doors? Do not save time to gain dollars, but to gain souls, to gain persons.

You may feel that you need to do cleaning on the weekend and that you need to mow your lawn. I agree with you. But sometimes you have to forget about your lawn. You promised the Lord to go out two hours a week. Do this first. Then use the rest of the time to mow the lawn. Take this way. If you would take my word, you may discover that you have more than two hours to go out. You may not realize how much you are enslaved in cleaning your home and in taking care of your lawn. Is there any pleasure in just taking care of your living and your house? But if you go out and within two hours baptize two persons, you will come back dancing. You will be addicted to that. You will have no patience to wait until next Saturday, but you will go the next day. You may even forget about the Lord's table to get others baptized.

Is the new way an impossible way? No, it is an altogether easy way. The Lord said that His yoke was easy (Matt. 11:30—KJV). The only problem is that we would not put our neck into His yoke. Absolute consecration is to mean business. A husband needs to take care of his wife and of his children and their education, but thank the Lord, it is not so hard to get our children educated in the United States. There is no excuse for not going out to bear fruit.

3. UNINTERRUPTED ABIDING IN THE LORD

To be in the Lord's new move is not just to learn the way from the training in Taipei. The way does not work without a right person. You must be a right person who always abides in the Lord. To abide in Him means to be one with Him. If you abide in Him, He promises to abide in you. You are in Him, and He is in you. You are just one with Him. Between you and Him there is no middle wall, no break, no interruption. When the Lord sent His disciples to go out, in a sense, that was He Himself going out. When the disciples went out to visit people, that was the Lord going out, so peace was with them. If you are a person abiding in the Lord all the time uninterruptedly, when you go out to knock on people's doors, that is the Lord's knocking. That is the Lord's gracious visitation. You bring the Lord with you, you send the Lord to them, and you share the Lord with them. Every chosen one, every God predestinated one, is a son of peace. They will be happy to receive what you would share with them.

The Mormons go out, but they do not have such a Lord. This depends on your uninterrupted abiding. In our training in Taipei, we do not only tell the trainees how to spend their time at the homes, but we also give them some basic points they have to build up. They must be persons abiding in the Lord twenty-four hours a day.

4. FULLY SATURATED WITH THE WORD

A word from a child in elementary school does not bear the weight as the same word from someone in junior high school. The same word out of a high schooler is weightier than that out of a junior higher. The word of a college graduate is much heavier and more full of weight than the same word from a high schooler. If the elders would take the new way and be trained to go out and do things according to the trained way, they will speak the same words from the same book, *The Mystery of Human Life,* but their word will be much weightier than the same word from the young ones.

Suppose a brother among us who is older and has the maturity and constitution in the divine life knocks on people's doors and sits down to speak with a young man only eighteen years of age. This young man will respect this brother's every word because he is aged, experienced, and learned. This brother's very person, the way he reads, and the way he speaks will catch him. If you know little about the truth and just go out with the little book to repeat it, there will not be much weight, much life, or much light. Thus, all the door-knockers should be fully saturated and soaked in the word.

I am a little concerned that many who have bought the Life-studies of the New Testament have just put them on their shelves. You have to get yourself soaked with the Life-studies. Every day at every available time you should read the messages. Do not put them on the shelf. It is good to scatter the Life-studies throughout your house. Turn to any page and read when you have even a little time. Every page has something. Every page is a pot of water. If you read it, you will get soaked and saturated. This is building up yourself to make yourself so qualified, full of the proper divine knowledge of the divine truth. Then you will be so weighty when you speak to people. This makes a great difference. This is not like two well-dressed young men from the Mormon church talking to people with no divine truth to convey. When we go out, we not only have a proper appearance, but we also have the Lord with us and have the building up of the word in our being as a person soaked in the holy truth. This makes a difference. This means a lot. A person who is weighty may go to a home and only sit while someone else talks, but even his sitting means something. All the angels will admire, and all the demons will shake at his presence. The angels will be happy with such a person.

5. PRAYER FOR THE FILLING OF BOTH THE ESSENTIAL AND ECONOMICAL SPIRIT

Acts 11:24 refers to the inward filling of the essential Spirit, and Acts 4:31 refers to the outward filling of the economical Spirit. In Acts 11 Barnabas was one filled with the Holy Spirit essentially and inwardly, so many people turned to the Lord. In Acts 4 the disciples were filled with the Holy Spirit outwardly and economically, so they spoke the word of God with boldness. To be filled essentially and economically with the Spirit always requires a thorough confession. We have to admit we are all sinful persons. We are regenerated, but we are in the body, in the flesh, and are still living on this earth with many dirty things. Physically speaking, how many times do you wash your hands? A doctor told us that doctors get sick less because they exercise to wash their hands frequently. If you want to avoid sickness, you had better wash your hands twelve times a day. You have to make a thorough confession many times a day. You may have had the filling of the Spirit, but your long face to your wife spoiled it, so you have to make a thorough confession to get yourself adjusted, to get yourself cleansed, to get yourself right with a right atmosphere; then you will once again enjoy the filling of the essential Spirit. Do this all the time.

Many of your prayers may only be for good jobs, good cars, or a good education. Those prayers make your person dirty. Forget about that. Use twenty minutes every day to make a thorough confession: "Lord, cleanse my mind, cleanse my thinking, cleanse my emotion, cleanse my loving of anything other than You. Lord, cleanse my will, my decision, my intention." Get yourself fully cleared up. You will surely have the Spirit filling you up inwardly, essentially, and outwardly, economically.

6. GOING WITH THE AUTHORITY OF CHRIST

If you have the previous five points, you are surely equipped, qualified, and ready to go with the power and the authority of Christ. To go to knock on doors means that you command the door to open. Sometimes you have to say, "Door, I knock; you open." When the man is there, give the commandment, not verbally but silently—"Man, listen to me. Let me in." While you are reading *The Mystery of Human Life,* tell the angels and demons that you are reading to this one with the authority of the ascended Christ. Many trainees in Taipei experienced this. They were surprised that the people were like lambs. They follow your directions to believe and be baptized. In the past when we talked to people, we did not have this realization. We did not exercise the very right we have been given. We had no intention to exercise our authority to command them to be baptized. Rather, we would tell the new ones that they could wait to be baptized. We gave up our right. Where was your authority to baptize new ones immediately into the Triune God?

Many of the trainees can testify that baptizing the new ones immediately after they received the Lord really worked and really made people happy. It changes people. In a Buddhist home, after the parents got baptized, with the little children standing by, they said to the idols of Buddha, "Buddha, we have Jesus now. We don't want you, and we don't need you. You have to go." Then the parents did away with the idols in the children's presence. This is wonderful! This is the authority of Christ. We go out with a position. We are the ambassadors sent by Him with authority to get people (2 Cor. 5:20). When you go out like this, all the demons will flee. The Devil will be gone, leaving the person under your hand just like a lamb.

THE WAY OF THE TRAINING MATCHED BY THE QUALIFICATIONS

The way of the training must be matched by these qualifications. The way of training can only work out something with qualified persons. When we talk about door-knocking, we are talking about this kind of door-knocking, not the kind practiced by the Mormons. You have the Lord, you have the word, you have the Spirit, and you have the Lord's authority. You go out with these four things. Do you not have the Lord? You are one with Him; you abide in Him. Do you not have the word? You are soaked and saturated with the word. Do you not have the Spirit? You are filled with both the essential and economical Spirit. Do you not have the authority of Christ? You are His ambassador. You have Christ the Lord, His word, His Spirit, and His authority to go out, so you are a fully equipped soldier. Who can resist you or stand against you? This is the way we go out.

I hope that the co-workers and elders would go out this way. Forget about giving messages in the halls. We have been doing that for years. That did not do much. Thank the Lord for these qualifications of door-knocking for fruit-bearing: aggressive desperation, absolute consecration, uninterrupted abiding in the Lord, full saturation with the word, prayer for the filling of both the essential and economical Spirit, and going with the authority of Christ.

Chapter Three

LIVING UNIQUELY FOR THE GOSPEL

1. To preach the high gospel: Acts 8:4-5
2. To teach the pure truth: 1 Tim. 2:4; 2 Tim. 2:2

THE DEFINITION OF THE GOSPEL

The gospel is Christ, who is the very embodiment of the processed Triune God, reaching us as the consummated Spirit, who is the consummation of the Triune God for our enjoyment. According to the truth, the gospel is the entire New Testament. Christians are used to saying that there are four Gospels, but Paul told us that the entire book of Romans is the gospel of God (1:1, 15). It includes the preaching of God, the condemnation of God upon fallen man, and the Body life, including the local churches in chapter sixteen. Have you ever received such a broad view of the definition of the gospel? Personally, the gospel is a wonderful person, and according to the truth, the gospel is the entire divine revelation of the twenty-seven books of the New Testament. God's New Testament economy is the gospel. We have to believe in such a gospel, preach such a gospel, and live uniquely for such a gospel. The consummated Spirit, who is God Himself reaching us, eventually has become the seven Spirits in Revelation (1:4; 4:5; 5:6). The seven Spirits are also a part of the gospel.

Truthwise, the gospel is the entire revelation of God's New Testament economy, including the first verse of Matthew, "Jesus Christ, Son of David, Son of Abraham," and including the last verse of Revelation, "The grace of the Lord Jesus be with all the saints. Amen." Jesus Christ, the Son of David, the Son of Abraham, in Matthew 1:1 is the very grace in

Revelation 22:21. In the first chapter of Matthew, the first chapter of the entire New Testament, we are also told that God was born into Mary (v. 20). The gospel includes God being born in Mary. The conception of the Savior was God's incarnation (John 1:14). The Gospel of Matthew also includes the church. In Matthew 16 Jesus Christ our Lord told His disciples He would build His church upon this rock, the revelation concerning Himself as the Christ, the Son of the living God (vv. 16-18). In Matthew 24:14 the Lord told us that the gospel of the kingdom of the heavens, which is the gospel of Matthew, will be preached to the whole inhabited earth.

Consider how much truth is in the Gospel of John, especially in chapters fourteen through sixteen, concerning the divine Trinity and concerning you and me as branches of the processed Triune God. Do you realize that we are the branches of the processed Triune God (15:5)? When I come to the details of John 14—16, I get excited. The Son is in the Father, the Father is in the Son (14:10-11), and eventually this Son is realized as the Spirit (14:17-20), so the entire Triune God comes to make an abode with us (14:23). Where are you now? You have to say that you are in the processed Triune God. And where is He now? In us. This mutual abode of us in the Triune God and He in us is the church, and this is the central point, the focus, of the Gospel of John.

LIVING UNIQUELY FOR THE GOSPEL

My intention is to impress you that in the universe and today on this earth there is something called the gospel which we are reminded and commanded to live for. The Lord commanded us to live for this gospel uniquely. What are we living on this earth for? Do we live for our profession or for our job to make a lot of money? What is man living for? Poor human society has so much activity but no goal. Do we have a goal? Our goal is the gospel, and our gospel is the Triune God processed to be the very Spirit within us as our salvation, as our life, as our life supply, and as our all-inclusive enjoyment.

What a wonder and what a glory to live uniquely for such a gospel. I have been living uniquely for this gospel for over fifty years. Hallelujah for this! It is worth it! When I was called by the Lord, my thinking was that God had called me to go to preach and teach in all the villages of my county, not even to my entire province. If I had done that all my life, I would have been more than happy. I never thought that I would be speaking in the United States and in other parts of the world to an international audience. By the Lord's mercy I am living uniquely for the gospel!

GOING WITH THE AUTHORITY OF CHRIST

At the end of the Gospel of Matthew, the Lord came as the very embodiment of the processed Triune God in resurrection and told us that all authority had been given to Him in heaven and on earth (28:18). The President of the United States sends ambassadors to many countries representing him with full authority, but why do we need this kind of authority, all authority in heaven and on earth? We need this authority to disciple the nations. All of us have to ask ourselves how many we have discipled. Have you believed in Him? Have you received Him? Do you have Him living in you? Are you one spirit with Him? Are you abiding in Him? Is He now abiding in you? Are you and He one? If you say yes to these questions, you have the authority in heaven and on earth to go! The worth and importance of the word "go" cannot be measured. Go, go, go! Go to Jerusalem first, then Judea, then Samaria, then to the remotest part of the earth (Acts 1:8). Go to all the homes in all the countries. Go to your cousins' homes, go to your in-laws' homes. Go to the homes to disciple the nations.

CUTTING OFF THE OLD WAY OF CHRISTIANITY BY GETTING INTO THE LORD'S NEW WAY

The hundred and twenty in Acts got the authority and received power when the Holy Spirit came upon them. This qualified and equipped them to go. They went, and great things happened. But following this the church became degraded. Degradation binds and restricts the resurrected and ascended Christ from accomplishing His heart's desire. Nearly everything revealed in the New Testament got bound, restricted and even killed over many centuries until the

Reformation with Martin Luther. Even Luther, though, did not get away from the background and the surrounding influence of Christianity. Then the Lord raised up the so-called mystics in the 1600s such as Madame Guyon, Father Fenelon, and Brother Lawrence in the Catholic church. Following this in the 1700s Zinzendorf was raised up and he practiced the church life to a certain extent. That was a great improvement. During the same time John Wesley was raised up as an individual giant to preach the gospel. Then in the next century Darby and his colleagues were raised up to have the brethren church practice. Their expounding of the Word of God opened up the Bible and brought much light.

William Law's improvement of mysticism helped Andrew Murray to the uttermost. From that point onward was the line of the inner life, which included Mrs. Penn-Lewis and all the great speakers in the Keswick Convention such as G. Campbell Morgan, A. J. Gordon, and S. D. Gordon. With T. Austin-Sparks the writings on the inner life reached their highest level. In the early 1900s Pentecostalism came out, and since the last century great preachers became prevailing such as C. H. Spurgeon, D. L. Moody, and Charles Finney. Today there are others.

These are major items of the Lord's move from the Reformation. All this has become history. The Reformation, however, eventually became a dead thing. Mysticism died out. The Moravian church life begun with Zinzendorf is far from what it once was. The inner life line died out. Today it is hard to even hear the term "inner life." What has been the result of the great evangelistic campaigns? They put out reports that thousands were gained by the Lord, but now where are they? There is hardly any increase in the statistics of the entire Christianity. The Assemblies of God have the highest rate of increase among the denominations, but it is only six percent yearly. This is a dying situation.

Now we must consider what way we should take. Should we take the Reformation way, the mystic way, the Moravian way, the Wesleyan way, the Brethren way, the inner life way, the Pentecostal way, or the giant preacher way? We have been under the influence of Christianity for years, and this influence is still surrounding us. It is hard for us to jump out. In 1927 I jumped out of Christianity, but I still had a Christianity "tail." That "tail" was with me, but it was reducing all the time. It took thirty years to get this "tail" to completely disappear. We must take the new way. The new way is first to cut off the "tail." Do not wait to reduce it. Do not say that since it took me thirty years to reduce the tail, you need more time. You can be faster. Jump into the new way to go out and visit people by door-knocking and setting up meetings in homes. Then your "tail" will be gone.

All the leavened items in Christianity are a part of the "tail." Much of the truth taught today is full of leaven. The birth of Christ has been leavened to a mass, Christmas, and the resurrection of Christ has been leavened to Easter. This is terrible. The way we have practiced in our meetings is still a part of the "tail." This is the old way to gather a congregation and to have a preacher, to encourage the congregation to come together every Sunday morning to hear a speaker.

You may think that there is nothing wrong for a gifted speaker to speak to you on the Lord's Day. But the entire practice of such a meeting is a killing. The Bible tells us that we are all members of the living Body of Christ (1 Cor. 12:27), and the Bible charges us as the members of Christ to function (Rom. 12:4-6). The first item of functioning is to preach the gospel, to reach the sinners, to visit them to bring them to Christ. Have we done this? Every Lord's Day we have had a big meeting occupying us. Actually this kind of meeting has killed our function. Many of us have been sitting in big meetings for years, but how much fruit did we bear?

THE SERIOUSNESS OF NOT BEARING FRUIT

Are you happy to remain in a barren situation for years? Second Peter indicates that it is possible for us to be idle and unfruitful, barren (1:8). Suppose tomorrow morning the Lord comes back. Then according to His word in Matthew 25, you will have to give Him an account of what you have been doing. What will you tell Him? Will you tell Him that you have had a good church life in your locality, that whatever He has given you is still here? Will you tell Him that He is a hard man, reaping where He did not sow and gathering where He did not scatter? What would the Lord say? Would the Lord say, "Well done, good and faithful slave...enter into the joy of your lord" (25:23)? Or would He call you an evil and slothful slave (25:26)? According to Matthew 25, where will He put you? Do not forget that the one who is put into outer darkness is the one who has received the real gift, one talent. This one is not only saved but also gifted. The Lord is real, He will really come back, and His word spoken in Matthew 25 will be fulfilled. This is a serious and solemn matter.

I am greatly burdened for those of you who have received my ministry for many years. I owe you this word. It is dangerous and risky not to bear fruit. I care about where you shall be—in the joy of your Lord or in outer darkness. After this fellowship, your blood shall be upon your own head and will not be required at my hand (Ezek. 33:4-9). One day you will stand before Him to give Him an account, especially concerning how much interest you have made for Him, that is, how many persons you have brought to Him. You received a talent from Him. He made a good investment in you. You must produce some interest. What have you been doing? I especially owe those of you who have been under my ministry for so many years and are not yet "on the track." Matthew 25 will be fulfilled.

In Matthew 28 the same Lord in His resurrection told us that He had received all authority in heaven and on earth, and this is now ours; so we must go to make some interest. He not only gave us the capital, the talent, but He also gave us all authority in heaven and on earth. We have no excuse. We have to go to produce interest, to bring forth fruit. He has given us His Spirit, His life, Himself as our talent, and His authority in heaven and on earth as our portion. We are more than capable, more than able, to get the interest because the entire universe will listen to us. In the United States there are still millions who are not Christians. We have to disciple them for the Lord. He told us to baptize them into the Triune God and teach them what He taught us. Then He promised us that He would be with us to the consummation of this age. Eventually, at the judgment seat of Christ (2 Cor. 5:10), we will have to give Him an account according to Matthew 25.

We must disciple the nations according to the Lord's new way. The first thing is to forget about the entire old way, to "cut off the tail." In October of 1984 I went to Taiwan for us to "cut off the tail" and to pick up the new way in a corporate way. The Lord's ordained way, revealed and recorded in the New Testament, is first to have the home meetings. Thus, we must go out to visit people in their homes. We are not just knocking on doors, but we are going out to reach people, to visit people. Actually, in Luke 10 the Lord sent the seventy to knock on doors to visit people and to go into their home and stay with them. Through my study in Taipei, I found out that this way works, but you must do it properly, not in a natural, old way, but in a trained, spiritual way, in the new way. The formula of the new way has been fully proven to work in the full-time training in Taipei over the last four months.

LIVING AS A JOB-DROPPING FULL-TIMER AND AS A WEEKLY DOOR-KNOCKER

We hope that one out of twenty saints will be a job-dropping full-timer and that one out of four saints will be a weekly door-knocker. Out of one hundred meeting in a certain locality there should be five job-dropping full-timers and twenty-five weekly door-knockers. Every full-timer who goes out at least five days for two to three hours a day can gain one every week. A team of three full-timers who goes out for five days, two to three hours a day, could knock on at least sixty doors. Out of the sixty doors they can gain four. Thus, each full-timer can gain one a week and fifty-two a year. Five full-timers then can gain at least two hundred and fifty in a year, a two and a half times increase. The twenty-five weekly door-knockers going out two or three hours weekly can each gain at least one within two months. If each one of the twenty-five gets six yearly, they will gain another one hundred and fifty. This amounts to a fourfold increase.

Each one of us needs to wake up to be serious, to live uniquely for the gospel. When you say that you live uniquely for the gospel, you have to consider the standard of your living. Regardless of how much money you make, it should not uplift the standard. The uplifted standard will not only waste your money but also waste your time. You will spend a lot of money and waste your time and energy. Then surely you will have no time to go out. If you have a bigger lawn, either you have to mow it or you have to hire others to do it. Thus, your money, energy, and time will all be wasted. Forget about having a higher standard of living. Every week save two hours to go out. I do not mean that you should not mow your lawn or take care of your house and belongings. But knocking on doors two or three hours a week is first. Let us all do this first. Then if there is any time left, go out a second time for two or three hours. We must live uniquely for the gospel. If you are faithful to the Lord by living uniquely for His gospel, the Lord will bless. He will bless your job or your business. He will take care of you. He will fulfill His promise in Matthew 6:33. If you seek His kingdom and His righteousness, He will give you His kingdom and His righteousness with an addition of all your daily necessities.

We have no excuse. We must learn to live on this earth uniquely for His gospel. As husbands, we care for our family, for our wife, and for our children and their education. We should take care of them, but only the living for the gospel should be the first. Suppose one hundred saints are living in a locality uniquely for the gospel. Some may be too old and it would be hard for them to go out to knock on doors. Some may be too young to go out. Forty percent may be either the old ones or the younger ones. Thus, there are still sixty who will have no excuse. Since you mean business to live uniquely for the gospel, you have to go out. All the other ways have died out. We must take the way to knock on doors. I believe that you even can gain one every month by going out two to three hours a week. Recently in a certain locality, thirty saints went out in ten teams of three, baptized seven, and set up twelve home meetings within an hour and a half. At this rate they could baptize twenty-eight within one month, which is approximately one saint baptizing one a month. Sixty saints gaining one per month results in seven hundred and twenty a year. You may say that not all of these will be faithful ones, but even if fifty percent of these are discounted that still means an increase of three hundred and sixty, which is more than a three and a half fold increase yearly. These statistics show that this is the way we must take.

PREACHING THE HIGH GOSPEL TO LEAD PEOPLE TO BELIEVE AND BE BAPTIZED

We need to go to preach the high gospel. The booklet we have published entitled *The Mystery of Human Life* really works. Thousands have been saved through this booklet. In it is the central way to present people the high gospel starting from God's creation of man. The parts of man are presented with a diagram of three circles showing man's spirit, soul, and body. It unveils God's intention to come into man's spirit so that man as a container, a vessel, may contain God. This high gospel of God's economy captures the thoughtful, educated people. After being educated, nearly every human being begins to think about the meaning of human life. Before the trainees presented the booklet, many said they were not interested. But the trainees said, "Just give us thirty seconds to read to you from *The Mystery of Human Life.*" This subject attracts people. After listening to the reading of the first page, many will say it is very good. When you hear "very good," that means that person is a son of peace. When he says "very good" or "not bad," that is the time for you to say, "Let's pray." Then you can turn to the back of the booklet and lead him to pray and call upon the name of the Lord. Following this, read the portion in the back of the booklet on baptism and show him Mark 16:16—believe and be baptized. Then lead him to be baptized in his bathtub. Exercise the authority in heaven and on earth that has been given to you. Regardless of this person's status, he will be a little lamb, going along with you to get changed and get into the water. In baptism we have a very prevailing prayer: "Lord, we place this one into You. We baptize him into the Triune God." This is the way to get people baptized within fifteen minutes.

I met a brother who is a sales manager over a region covering half of the United States. Under his management are one thousand five hundred salesmen. He told me that the way to make sales is exactly the same as our instructions to knock on doors. I was happy to hear this. He even said that there were probably some points that they could learn of us. In his training of people to sell door-to-door, the first point is the proper dress and behavior. He said you should neither dress too casually nor too extravagantly. We instructed the trainees in Taipei in the same way related to their appearance. The second point with his salesmen is to have a preparation time. Even their salesmen before going out have a time to come together to have a little conference to get themselves prepared. We shared that we need to get ourselves prepared by prayer before going out. Then they advise to keep the approach short. Do not have a long talk. A long talk will annul the deal. We have shared the same thing. Then this brother advises his salesmen to follow the training they offer. It is specific and it works. As we have pointed out, this means not to speak your own words, but to speak every word according to the training's instructions.

In doing anything successfully there is a certain principle. You must get the principle and learn it. Do not think that to knock on doors to get people baptized is easy. No, it has its principle. There are principles in learning how to play the piano. Now we are endeavoring to live uniquely for the gospel, and no other way is prevailing but the Lord's new way. This has been proven by Christian history for centuries. We studied many of the practices of the past and tried them. We had many of the books of the leading mystics translated into Chinese close to fifty years ago. We studied nearly all of the leading books of the inner life. I learned a lot from them. I was with the Brethren, and Brother Nee studied many books put out by the Brethren teachers. We even tried some items of the Pentecostal movement and found out that it was not profitable. We must cut off "the tail" of the leaven of Christianity to have a new way, and the new way is fully ordained by God and recorded in the Bible. It is here now for us to practice. We have tried this way, and it works.

If each one of you would rise up and go out for some time once a week for two or three hours, everyone will get one a month or twelve a year. What an increase we will have! I must be faithful to tell you this. After telling you this, you bear the responsibility. We must visit people to share with them the high gospel, that is, the Triune God Himself to be our life and content.

Our sharing of the gospel with people is to lead them to believe and be baptized. In the Bible not one who repented and believed was told to wait for some time to be baptized. Every case was that they repented, believed, and were baptized (Acts 8:36-38; 16:14-15, 31-33; 22:16). This is the biblical way. When people repent and believe, that is the right time for you to exercise your authority to authorize their baptism. The Holy Spirit honors this and confirms this. This baptism could never be a ritual. But if you ask people to wait four months and then baptize them, that baptism will become a ritual and not bear any significance in the power of the Spirit. We do not need to wait to get into the meeting hall's baptistery. Right away from the living room, we get them into the bathroom to exercise the power of the Spirit in baptism. What a big difference! If you would take this way and practice faithfully to go out three hours weekly for four weeks a month, I assure you that you can gain one person.

SETTING UP MEETINGS IN THE HOMES TO TEACH THE PURE TRUTH

Following this, set up a meeting in their home to teach them the pure truth by first using the *New Life Lessons.* These lessons teach them how to start their Christian life. Then following these we must use the *Truth Lessons.* The *Truth Lessons* were written in a way to teach the believers the truth in a very good sequence and line. Now we have the first three volumes in English. If you only give the new ones a sheet of paper with points of the truth on it, they may not respect it very much. After using it, it might be put aside. However, if you would recommend these books, telling them that this series will be in four levels for four years and that each level has four volumes, they will be impressed. When they see a set of books like this, they will respect them, keep them, and treasure them.

You do not need to teach them lesson by lesson as we have done in the past one or two years. Use the line of growing in life in volume three that speaks concerning the real condition of a sinner, Christ's redemption, forgiveness, regeneration, and justification, all in detail. You do not need to use the entire lesson. Circle or mark out certain paragraphs and teach them these certain paragraphs in about twenty minutes or at the most thirty minutes. Give them an assignment, telling them that they have to read the rest of the paragraphs.

You have to get yourself familiar with all the truth lessons. Then you can tell them that this set of *Truth Lessons* is in a good order. If they want to know where the Bible came from, there is a truth lesson to tell them. This will not be a lesson book to them, but their reading material. It is written in such a way that everybody can read it. They may not understand certain phrases, or terminology temporarily, but gradually they will pick them up.

If they have a question about who Jesus Christ is, show them a lesson telling them who Jesus Christ is. Ask them to read that lesson with much prayer. Then they will get the full knowledge of Jesus Christ. If they want to know what the church is, show them a lesson on the church. In other words, give them a little portion for your teaching, but assign them to read the rest of the paragraphs of a certain lesson.

They also need a complete Bible including the Old Testament. I still like to recommend the American Standard Version. Although it is an old translation, it is still quite good. Also encourage them to get a copy of the Recovery Version of the New Testament because they can read all the notes. After this, recommend to them our publications, such as the rainbow booklets, the Life-study Messages, and the many other small books. Encourage them to get these publications gradually and lead them to grow into the habit of reading the Bible and the spiritual books.

THE NEW BAPTIZED ONES LEARNING TO PREACH THE GOSPEL, TAKE CARE OF THEIR MEETING, AND TEACH THE TRUTH

After you visit them two or three times, they will join you to knock on doors. They will learn to preach the gospel. In Taipei we even saw some right after baptism following the trainees to go out to baptize people. After half a year they will learn how to take care of the meeting. From the first day, you must tell them that this is their meeting, and you are only coming to help. They should function to take care of the meeting. They must learn how to pray, how to sing, how to call a hymn, how to read the Bible, and how to do many things. After six months, they will learn how to take care of the meeting. Then after another two years, they will be able to teach others. All the new baptized ones will learn to preach the gospel, to take care of their meeting, and to teach the truth. There will be thousands of homes where everyone can function, will function, and does function because they have been ushered into such a practice. Then they will spontaneously be led into the knowledge of the church and the practice of the real church life.

THE WHOLE CHURCH COMING TOGETHER

If in a certain locality the number is quite big, occasionally the whole church can come together once a month or once every two months. If you do not have a big hall, you can rent a place to get all the saints together. The church in Taipei has decided this year to collect all the saints together once a month, renting a stadium that can take thirteen thousand. Last November we had over thirteen thousand meeting together in this stadium. We expect to have in the next two or three months at least ten thousand meeting there for the whole day. For the rest of the days they can all meet in the homes. This is the way to have the church life.

THE LORD APPOINTING US TO GO FORTH AND BEAR FRUIT AND THAT OUR FRUIT SHOULD REMAIN

John 15:16 says, "You did not choose Me, but I chose you, and I appointed you that you should go forth and bear fruit, and that your fruit should remain." In this verse there are some words which are quite crucial. The first word is "appointed." We did not choose ourselves, but He chose us. We have no choice in the matter of being a branch of Christ, the vine, because He caught us. He chose us and appointed us to bear fruit. To bear fruit is the Lord's appointment, His assignment. He did not assign us to do anything else. He appointed us to bear fruit. The Lord charged us to go forth and bear fruit. Can a branch go? The branches of a physical tree do not go. But we are not only living branches, but also movable branches. We have to go. This indicates that we have to reach people.

Our mistake in the past was that we did not go, yet we asked people to come. We took the wrong way. We asked people to come to our love feasts (Jude 12) instead of going to people. It is very hard for many to come to us, but when we go, we can reach people everywhere. In Luke 10 the Lord told us He sent us as lambs in the midst of wolves, yet among the wolves there are some sons of peace (vv. 3-6). By going to them, knocking on doors, eventually we find out who are the sons of peace. God chose and predestinated them before the foundation of the world, yet today they were born into the flock of wolves. Who knows who is a son of God, a son of peace? The only way to know them is to knock on doors. By your knocking on doors, you will discover who is a son of peace, a son of God. We have to go because we have been appointed to go.

The Lord says that we should go forth and bear fruit and that our fruit should remain. In the past we took the wrong way. Occasionally people came to us and they believed and were baptized, but they did not remain because nobody took care of them. This is like a mother delivering a child, and then leaving her newborn baby without any care. How could she expect this baby to remain? The Lord has shown us the way for our fruit to remain. We do not just go out to reach people by knocking on their doors and bringing them into the Triune God through their believing and baptism. After this, we immediately set up a home meeting in their home. To set up a home meeting is to set up a shelter to protect this new babe. The farmers protect the fruit in their orchard. Peaches that are ripe and have just been picked need to be covered. Otherwise, the birds may eat them. This covering helps the fruit to remain. Likewise, to set up a meeting in a baptized one's home is to set up a shelter. Then under the shelter you go back to them regularly to feed them. Surely they will be protected, they will be fed, and they will remain. This is the secret of having remaining fruit.

The picture the Lord has shown us concerning the church life is not to ask people to come to attend our meetings. But, the picture as revealed in the Bible is that we all have to go. To knock on doors really means to visit people in a practical way. Knocking on doors really means visiting. The Lord Jesus took the lead. He came down from the heavens to visit people. He did a great deal of visitation, so we should follow Him to visit people. We should go to bring forth fruit, go to disciple the nations, and go to preach the gospel. After we bring people to the Lord through baptism, we immediately set up a meeting in their home, so we continue to go. The first time we go to baptize them, the second time we go to feed them, the third time we go to teach them, and the fourth time we go to nourish them. Your going will always be a sheltering, feeding, teaching, and nourishing. By our going again and again to these new ones, they will grow.

Very few babies die after being delivered today in the United States because after the delivery the modern hospitals have the best way to protect, shepherd, and feed them. Premature or sick babies are even put in an incubator for protection and nourishment. We should keep going back to the new ones again and again. We meet with them, not in the hall but in their homes. This kind of meeting in the homes will shepherd them and will keep us alive. To come to the hall to big meetings week after week on the one hand helped us and on the other hand killed our function. Some who came into the church life were initially very active, but eventually after attending big meetings for a length of time they became dormant and out of function with no interest and no incentive. But if we have new ones to take care of, this will be our incentive.

Our trainees have been trained not to spend too long a time at a home meeting, only twenty or at the most thirty minutes. You have to take care of two home meetings in one hour or four home meetings in two hours. When you go to the home meetings you have set up to visit all these new ones, you will be happy. Most of the nurses in the hospital who take care of the newborn babes are happy. The new ones that you have to nourish will become an incentive to you to encourage you to work for the Lord. What happiness this will be!

Then maybe once a month or every two months, the whole church can come together. What a church life that would be! How will you feel when you see forty-five of your fruit in the meeting whom you baptized in the bathtubs? Glorious! Then when the Lord comes back, you will be bold to go to Him. All the ones you brought to the Lord will be your joy and your crown at the Lord's coming (1 Thes. 2:19-20). This will change, revolutionize, and transfer the church life into another realm. This all depends on our faithfulness.

Today we say we live Christ but by what way? Just by having morning watch, reading the Bible in our home, and coming to the meetings on the Lord's day? If we are living Christ, we will release Christ out of our being to bear fruit, and our fruit will remain. This is the real church life and the real Christian life.

PUTTING THE NEW WAY INTO PRACTICE TO SEE THE LORD'S BLESSING

Your success in the new way depends upon your practice. With the right practice, you will eventually discover all the necessary details. But I assure you the blessing will be there with you. The Lord will bless your knocking on doors. The Lord will bless your setting up home meetings, and He will bless all the home meetings if you will practice this way according to what I have instructed. Do not use any natural way. The natural way will not work. Go strictly according to the instruction of the Lord's new way. If you will be faithful to put all these things into practice, there will be some among you to help you to understand all the fine details.

I believe everyone can bring in one a month and that the home meetings will be very much blessed. The new ones will learn to go out knocking on doors, to take care of their home meetings, and after two or three years to teach others. Then you have to seek the Lord's leading when to set up the Lord's table with them. Maybe after a certain time they can have the Lord's table meeting. You have to teach them how to live the Christian life, including their giving something to the Lord. Do not use the old way; everything must be new. Then you will see the Lord's blessing. This is the way for the Lord to carry out His eternal economy that He may prepare His bride for His second coming.

About the Author

Witness Lee was born in 1905 in northern China and raised in a Christian family. At age 19 he was fully captured for Christ and immediately consecrated himself to preach the gospel for the rest of his life. Early in his service, he met Watchman Nee, a renowned preacher, teacher, and writer. Witness Lee labored together with Watchman Nee under his direction. In 1934 Watchman Nee entrusted Witness Lee with the responsibility for his publication operation, called the Shanghai Gospel Bookroom.

Prior to the Communist takeover in 1949, Witness Lee was sent by Watchman Nee and his other co-workers to Taiwan to ensure that the things delivered to them by the Lord would not be lost. Watchman Nee instructed Witness Lee to continue the former's publishing operation abroad as the Taiwan Gospel Bookroom, which has been publicly recognized as the publisher of Watchman Nee's works outside China. Witness Lee's work in Taiwan manifested the Lord's abundant blessing. From a mere 350 believers, newly fled from the mainland, the churches in Taiwan grew to 20,000 in five years.

In 1962 Witness Lee felt led of the Lord to come to the United States, settling in California. During his 35 years of service in the U.S., he ministered in weekly meetings and weekend conferences, delivering several thousand spoken messages. Much of his speaking has since been published as over 400 titles. Many of these have been translated into over fourteen languages. He gave his last public conference in February 1997 at the age of 91.

He leaves behind a prolific presentation of the truth in the Bible. His major work, *Life-study of the Bible,* comprises over 25,000 pages of commentary on every book of the Bible from the perspective of the believers' enjoyment and experience of God's divine life in Christ through the Holy Spirit. Witness Lee was the chief editor of a new translation of the New Testament into Chinese called the Recovery Version and directed the translation of the same into English. The Recovery Version also appears in a number of other languages. He provided an extensive body of footnotes, outlines, and spiritual cross references. A radio broadcast of his messages can be heard on Christian radio stations in the United States. In 1965 Witness Lee founded Living Stream Ministry, a non-profit corporation, located in Anaheim, California, which officially presents his and Watchman Nee's ministry.

Witness Lee's ministry emphasizes the experience of Christ as life and the practical oneness of the believers as the Body of Christ. Stressing the importance of attending to both these matters, he led the churches under his care to grow in Christian life and function. He was unbending in his conviction that God's goal is not narrow sectarianism but the Body of Christ. In time, believers began to meet simply as the church in their localities in response to this conviction. In recent years a number of new churches have been raised up in Russia and in many eastern European countries.

OTHER BOOKS PUBLISHED BY
Living Stream Ministry

Titles by Witness Lee:

Abraham—Called by God	0-7363-0359-6
The Experience of Life	0-87083-417-7
The Knowledge of Life	0-87083-419-3
The Tree of Life	0-87083-300-6
The Economy of God	0-87083-415-0
The Divine Economy	0-87083-268-9
God's New Testament Economy	0-87083-199-2
The World Situation and God's Move	0-87083-092-9
Christ vs. Religion	0-87083-010-4
The All-inclusive Christ	0-87083-020-1
Gospel Outlines	0-87083-039-2
Character	0-87083-322-7
The Secret of Experiencing Christ	0-87083-227-1
The Life and Way for the Practice of the Church Life	0-87083-785-0
The Basic Revelation in the Holy Scriptures	0-87083-105-4
The Crucial Revelation of Life in the Scriptures	0-87083-372-3
The Spirit with Our Spirit	0-87083-798-2
Christ as the Reality	0-87083-047-3
The Central Line of the Divine Revelation	0-87083-960-8
The Full Knowledge of the Word of God	0-87083-289-1
Watchman Nee—A Seer of the Divine Revelation ...	0-87083-625-0

Titles by Watchman Nee:

How to Study the Bible	0-7363-0407-X
God's Overcomers	0-7363-0433-9
The New Covenant	0-7363-0088-0
The Spiritual Man 3 volumes	0-7363-0269-7
Authority and Submission	0-7363-0185-2
The Overcoming Life	1-57593-817-0
The Glorious Church	0-87083-745-1
The Prayer Ministry of the Church	0-87083-860-1
The Breaking of the Outer Man and the Release ...	1-57593-955-X
The Mystery of Christ	1-57593-954-1
The God of Abraham, Isaac, and Jacob	0-87083-932-2
The Song of Songs	0-87083-872-5
The Gospel of God 2 volumes	1-57593-953-3
The Normal Christian Church Life	0-87083-027-9
The Character of the Lord's Worker	1-57593-322-5
The Normal Christian Faith	0-87083-748-6
Watchman Nee's Testimony	0-87083-051-1

Available at

Christian bookstores, or contact Living Stream Ministry
2431 W. La Palma Ave. • Anaheim, CA 92801
1-800-549-5164 • www.livingstream.com